RAND McNALLY

Los Angeles & Vicinity

Regional *EasyFinder*®

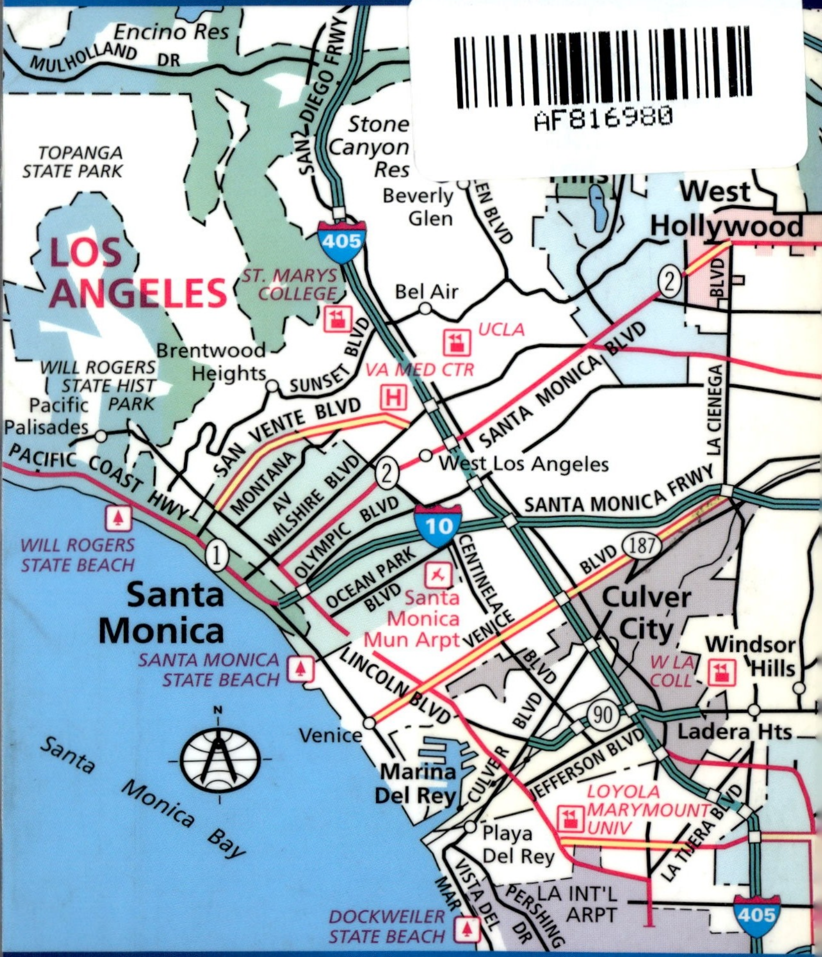

- ✔ Easy to handle
- ✔ Easy to fold
- ✔ Durable – won't tear
- ✔ Write on – wipe off

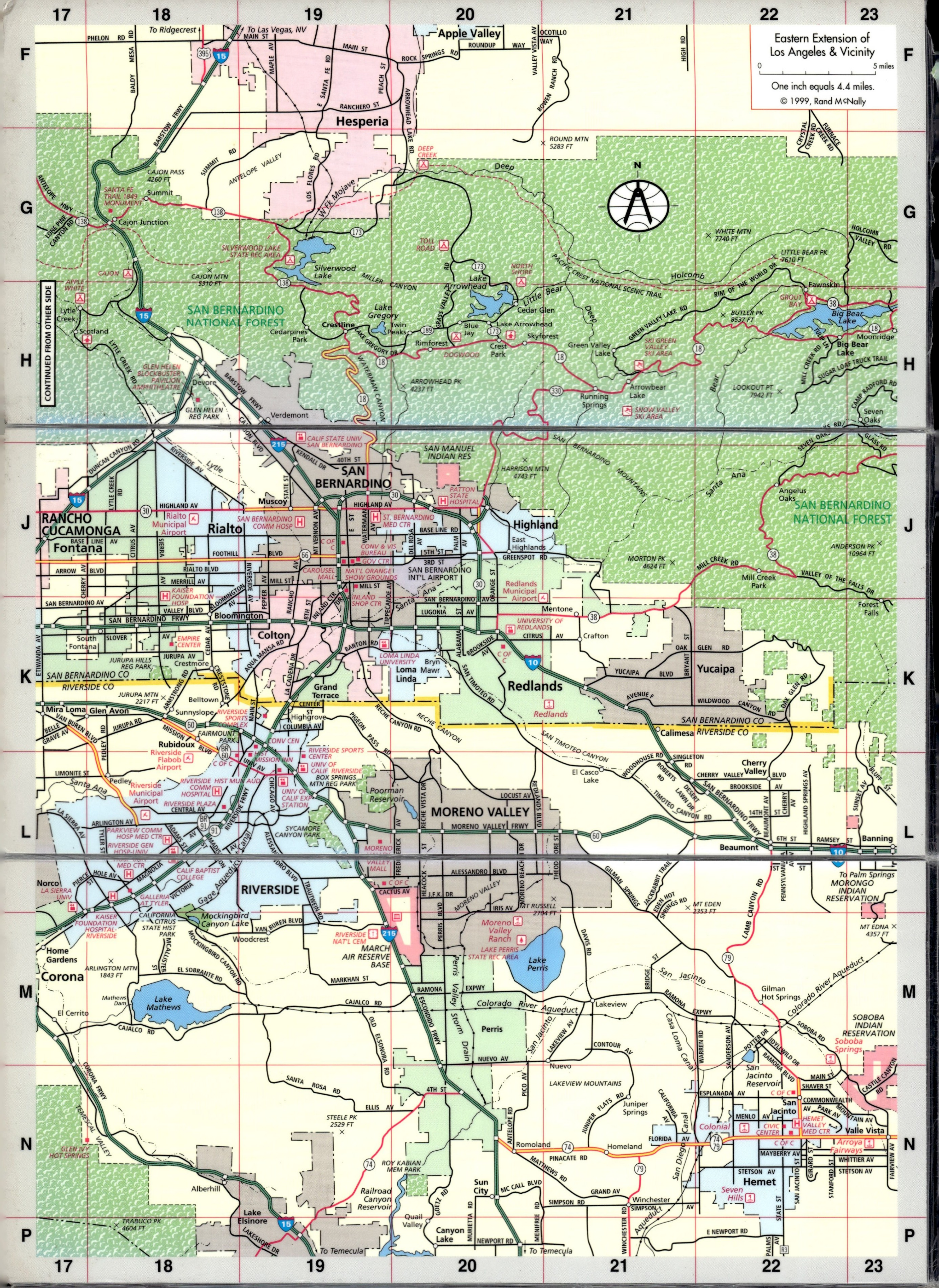
Eastern Extension of
Los Angeles & Vicinity
0
5 miles
One inch equals 4.4 miles.
© 1999, Rand McNally
17
18
19
20
21
22
23
F
G
H
J
K
L
M
N
P
CONTINUED FROM OTHER SIDE
To Ridgecrest
To Las Vegas, NV
Apple Valley
PHELON RD
MAIN ST
ROCK SPRINGS RD
ROUNDUP
WAY
OCOTILLO WAY
BOWEN RANCH RD
HIGH RD
BALDY MESA RD
MAPLE AV
E SANTA FE RD
PEACH ST
ARROWHEAD LAKE RD
RANCHERO ST
Hesperia
BARSTOW FRWY
ROUND MTN 5283 FT
CRYSTAL CREEK RD
FURNACE CREEK RD
DEEP CREEK
Deep
CAJON PASS 4260 FT
Summit
SUMMIT RD
ANTELOPE VALLEY RD
LOS FLORES RD
W Fk Mojave
ANTELOPE HWY
SANTA FE TRAIL 1849 MONUMENT
Cajon Junction
LONE PINE CANYON RD
SILVERWOOD LAKE STATE REC AREA
Silverwood Lake
TOLL ROAD
WHITE MTN 7740 FT
HOLCOMB VALLEY RD
LITTLE BEAR PK 7610 FT
PACIFIC CREST NATIONAL SCENIC TRAIL
Holcomb
RIM OF THE WORLD DR
Fawnskin
CAJON
CAJON MTN 5310 FT
MILLER CANYON
Lake Arrowhead
NORTH SHORE
Little Bear
APPLE WHITE
Lytle Creek
SAN BERNARDINO NATIONAL FOREST
Lake Gregory
GRASS VALLEY RD
Cedar Glen
Lake Arrowhead
GREEN VALLEY LAKE RD
GROUT BAY
Big Bear Lake
Scotland
Cedarpines Park
Crestline
Twin Peaks
Blue Jay
Skyforest
Deep
BUTLER PK 8537 FT
Moonridge
LAKE GREGORY DR
Rimforest
Crest Park
DOGWOOD
Green Valley Lake
SKI GREEN VALLEY SKI AREA
Big Bear Lake
LYTLE CREEK RD
GLEN HELEN BLOCKBUSTER PAVILION AMPHITHEATRE
Devore
WATERMAN CANYON
ARROWHEAD PK 4237 FT
Arrowbear Lake
Running Springs
MILL CREEK RD
SUGAR LOAF TRUCK TRAIL
LOOKOUT PT 7942 FT
Bear
CAMP RADFORD RD
GLEN HELEN REG PARK
BARSTOW FRWY
Verdemont
SNOW VALLEY SKI AREA
Seven Oaks
CALIF STATE UNIV SAN BERNARDINO
SAN MANUEL INDIAN RES
SEVEN OAKS RD
GLASS RD
DUNCAN CANYON RD
RIVERSIDE AV
Lytle
KENDALL DR
40TH ST
SAN BERNARDINO
HARRISON MTN 4743 FT
SAN BERNARDINO MOUNTAINS
Santa Ana
Angelus Oaks
SAN BERNARDINO NATIONAL FOREST
LYTLE CREEK RD
HIGHLAND AV
Muscoy
STATE ST
PATTON STATE HOSPITAL
RANCHO CUCAMONGA
Rialto Municipal Airport
Rialto
SAN BERNARDINO COMM HOSP
ST. BERNARDINE MED CTR
Highland
East Highlands
BASE LINE AV
Fontana
CITRUS AV
SIERRA AV
FOOTHILL BLVD
MT VERNON AV
C OF C
CONV & VIS BUREAU
GOV CTR
WATERMAN AV
DEL ROSA AV
PALM AV
5TH ST
3RD ST
GREENSPOT RD
ANDERSON PK 10964 FT
MORTON PK 4624 FT
MILL CREEK RD
Mill Creek Park
VALLEY OF THE FALLS DR
ARROW BLVD
RIALTO BLVD
MERRILL AV
CHERRY AV
CAROUSEL MALL
NAT'L ORANGE SHOW GROUNDS
SAN BERNARDINO INT'L AIRPORT
MILL ST
KAISER FOUNDATION HOSP
INLAND SHOP CTR
Redlands Municipal Airport
ORANGE ST
SAN BERNARDINO AV
VALLEY BLVD
Bloomington
BLOOMINGTON AV
PEPPER AV
RANCHO AV
Mentone
Forest Falls
SAN BERNARDINO FRWY
LUGONIA AV
UNIVERSITY OF REDLANDS
Crafton
ETIWANDA AV
South Fontana
SLOVER AV
EMPIRE CENTER
CEDAR AV
Colton
AQUA MANSA RD
BARTON RD
LOMA LINDA UNIVERSITY
Loma Linda
Bryn Mawr
ALABAMA ST
BROOKSIDE AV
CITRUS AV
C OF C
OAK
GLEN RD
BRYANT ST
YUCAIPA BLVD
Yucaipa
JURUPA HILLS REG PARK
JURUPA AV
Crestmore
SAN BERNARDINO CO
RIVERSIDE CO
LA CADENA DR
Grand Terrace
SAN TIMOTEO RD
Redlands
AVENUE F
WILDWOOD CANYON RD
OAK GLEN RD
JURUPA MTN 2217 FT
ARMSTRONG RD
Belltown
CENTER ST
Mira Loma
Glen Avon
Sunnyslope
RIVERSIDE SPORTS COMPLEX
Highgrove
COLUMBIA AV
RECHE CANYON RD
Calimesa
SAN BERNARDINO CO
RIVERSIDE CO
BELLE GRAVE AV
VAN BUREN BLVD
JURUPA RD
MISSION BLVD
FAIRMOUNT PARK
PIGEON PASS RD
Rubidoux
CONV CEN
Riverside Flabob Airport
HIST MISSION INN
RIVERSIDE SPORTS CENTER
SAN TIMOTEO CANYON
SINGLETON RD
WOODHOUSE RD
LIMONITE ST
C OF C
UNIV OF CALIF RIVERSIDE
El Casco Lake
ROBERTS RD
DESERT LAWN DR
Cherry Valley
Pedley
BOX SPRINGS MTN REG PARK
CHERRY VALLEY BLVD
BROOKSIDE AV
Santa Ana
Riverside Municipal Airport
RIVERSIDE HIST MUN AUD
RIVERSIDE COMM HOSPITAL
UNIV OF CALIF EXP STATION
Poorman Reservoir
LOCUST AV
TIMOTEO CANYON RD
SAN BERNARDINO FRWY
RIVERSIDE PLAZA
CENTRAL AV
REDLANDS BLVD
14TH ST
HIGHLAND SPRINGS AV
SUNSET AV
BLUFF ST
LA SIERRA AV
ARLINGTON AV
CHICAGO AV
SYCAMORE CANYON PARK
MORENO VALLEY
MORENO VALLEY FRWY
BEAUMONT AV
6TH ST
RAMSEY ST
Banning
PARKVIEW COMM HOSP MED CTR
RIVERSIDE GEN HOSP-UNIV MED CTR
TYLER ST
ADAMS ST
RIVERSIDE FRWY
ALESSANDRO BLVD
MORENO VALLEY MALL
RECHE VISTA DR
Beaumont
Norco
LA SIERRA UNIV
PIERCE ST
HOLE AV
MAGNOLIA AV
CALIF BAPTIST COLLEGE
Gage Aqueduct
RIVERSIDE
TRAUTWEIN RD
FREDERICK
HEACOCK ST
ALESSANDRO BLVD
MORENO BEACH DR
THEODORE ST
GILMAN SPRINGS RD
JACKRABBIT TRAIL
To Palm Springs
MORONGO INDIAN RESERVATION
KAISER FOUNDATION HOSPITAL-RIVERSIDE
GALLERIA AT TYLER
VICTORIA
CALIFORNIA CITRUS STATE HIST PARK
Mockingbird Canyon Lake
VAN BUREN BLVD
CACTUS AV
C OF C
J.F.K. DR
MORENO VALLEY
IRIS AV
MT RUSSELL 2704 FT
EDEN HOT SPRINGS RD
MT EDEN 2353 FT
LAMB CANYON RD
PENNSYLVANIA AV
MT EDNA 4357 FT
Home Gardens
Corona
ARLINGTON MTN 1843 FT
MCALLISTER ST
Woodcrest
MOCKINGBIRD CANYON RD
EL SOBRANTE RD
RIVERSIDE NAT'L CEM
MARCH AIR RESERVE BASE
PERRIS BLVD
Moreno Valley Ranch
LAKE PERRIS STATE REC AREA
Lake Perris
DAVIS RD
BRIDGE ST
San Jacinto
Gilman Hot Springs
Colorado River Aqueduct
Mathews Dam
Lake Mathews
MARKHAN ST
RAMONA EXPWY
Perris Valley Storm Drain
Lakeview
RAMONA EXPWY
El Cerrito
CAJALCO RD
Colorado River Aqueduct
SOBOBA RD
SOBOBA INDIAN RESERVATION
Soboba Springs
OLD ELSONORA RD
ESCONDIDO FRWY
Perris
San Jacinto
LAKEVIEW AV
CONTOUR AV
Casa Loma Canal
WARREN RD
SANDERSON AV
POTTER DR
IDYLLWILD DR
RAMONA BLVD
San Jacinto Reservoir
MAIN ST
SHAVER ST
CASTILE CANYON RD
CORONA FRWY
NUEVO AV
Nuevo
LAKEVIEW MOUNTAINS
SANTA ROSA RD
4TH ST
PICO AV
JUNIPER FLATS RD
Juniper Springs
CALIFORNIA AV
San Diego Canal
ESPLANADA AV
C OF C
COMMONWEALTH AV
San Jacinto
PARK AV
MOUNTAIN AV
TEMESCAL VALLEY
ELLIS AV
STEELE PK 2529 FT
ANTELOPE RD
MENLO AV
HEMET VALLEY MED CTR
Valle Vista
GLEN IVY HOT SPRINGS
Romoland
Homeland
FLORIDA AV
Colonial
CIVIC CENTER
C OF C
Arroya Fairways
PINACATE RD
MAYBERRY AV
WHITTIER AV
ROY KABIAN MEM PARK
MATHEWS RD
GIRARD ST
STANFORD ST
FAIRVIEW AV
Alberhill
Railroad Canyon Reservoir
Sun City
MC CALL BLVD
GRAND AV
STETSON AV
Hemet
STETSON AV
Seven Hills
SAN JACINTO ST
Winchester
SIMPSON RD
Aqueduct
Lake Elsinore
TRABUCO PK 4604 FT
Quail Valley
GOETZ RD
Canyon Lake
MURRIETA RD
MENIFREE RD
WINCHESTER RD
E NEWPORT RD
STATE ST
NEWPORT RD
LAKESHORE DR
To Temecula
To Temecula
PALMS

6 7 8 9 10 11

EasyFinder® U.S. Patent No. 5,868,429. Additional patents pending. Canadian Industrial Design Reg. No. 76,725.

6 7 8 9 10 11

12
13
14
15
16
17
F
G
H
J
K
L
M
N
P
Q
R
ANGELES NATIONAL FOREST
SAN GABRIEL MOUNTAINS
ANGELES CREST HWY
PACIFIC CREST NATIONAL SCENIC TRAIL
Valyermo
Phelon
Wrightwood
BARE MTN 6388 FT
PACIFIC MTN 7124 FT
STRAWBERRY PK 6164 FT
SAN GABRIEL PK 6161 FT
MT WILSON 5710 FT
MT WILSON OBSERVATORY
THROOP PK 9134 FT
MT SAN ANTONIO 10064 FT
CUCAMONGA PK 8859 FT
SAN GABRIEL WILDERNESS
CUCAMONGA WILDERNESS
Tujunga
Cogswell Reservoir
San Gabriel Res
Morris Reservoir
Mount Baldy
Lytle Creek
Scotland
LOS ANGELES CO
SAN BERNARDINO CO
Altadena
Monrovia
PASADENA
Sierra Madre
Arcadia
Duarte
Azusa
Glendora
San Dimas
La Verne
Claremont
UPLAND
RANCHO CUCAMONGA
Fontana
Alta Loma
San Marino
Temple City
San Gabriel
ALHAMBRA
EL MONTE
Baldwin Park
Irwindale
Covina
Charter Oak
POMONA
Montclair
ONTARIO
ONTARIO INTL AIRPORT
Guasti
Monterey Park
Rosemead
South El Monte
West Covina
La Puente
Valinda
Walnut
Montebello
Pico Rivera
City of Industry
South San Jose Hills
Diamond Bar
Chino
Chino Airport
Mira Loma
Glen Avon
Hacienda Hts
Whittier
Rowland Heights
La Habra Hts
Los Serranos
Chino Hills
Sleepy Hollow
South Whittier
Santa Fe Springs
Los Nietos
LOS ANGELES CO
ORANGE CO
CONTINUED ON OTHER SIDE
SAN BERNARDINO CO
RIVERSIDE CO
Downey
La Mirada
La Habra
Brea
RIVERSIDE
Norco
Bellflower
Norwalk
Cerritos
FULLERTON
Placentia
Yorba Linda
CHINO HILLS STATE PARK
Corona Municipal Airport
Coronita
Home Gardens
Artesia
Lakewood
Buena Park
La Palma
ANAHEIM
Corona
El Cerrito
Hawaiian Gardens
Cypress
Olive
Villa Park
LONG BEACH
Los Alamitos
Rossmoor
Stanton
GARDEN GROVE
ORANGE
Orange Park Acres
El Modena
Cowan Heights
Lemon Heights
CLEVELAND NATIONAL FOREST
SIERRA PK 3045 FT
Santiago Res (Irvine Lake)
Westminster
Midway City
SANTA ANA
Tustin
Red Hill
Silverado
Modjeska
Seal Beach
US NAVAL WEAPONS STATION
HUNTINGTON BEACH
Huntington Harbor
Sunset Beach
Bolsa Chica Wetlands (ECOLOGICAL RES)
BOLSA CHICA STATE BEACH
Fountain Valley
SANTA ANA MCAS
EL TORO
MCAS
SANTIAGO PK 5687 FT
Costa Mesa
John Wayne Airport (Orange Co)
IRVINE
Lake Forest
Lake Mission Viejo
Rancho Santa Margarita
Coto De Caza
HUNTINGTON STATE BEACH
Upper Newport Bay
Newport Beach
Balboa
Corona Del Mar
CORONA DEL MAR STATE BEACH
Mission Viejo
Laguna Hills
FERRY TO CATALINA ISLAND
Crystal Cove
CRYSTAL COVE STATE PARK
Emerald Bay
Laguna Beach
Laguna Niguel
Gulf of Santa Catalina
South Laguna
San Juan Capistrano
Dana Point
DOHENY STATE BEACH
Capistrano Beach
San Clemente
To San Diego
ORANGE CO
SAN DIEGO CO
SAN ONOFRE STATE PARK

STREET INDEX

1st St ... L-22,N-13-14
2nd St ... L-17
3rd St ... J-20
4th St ... K-16,N-20
5th St ... J-20
6th St ... L-17-22,M-17
7th Av ... F-19
8th St ... K-19
9th St ... N-10
14th St ... L-22
17th St ... N-14
19th St ... J-16
40th St ... J-19
68th St ... L-17
96th St E ... F-13
190th St ... M-10

A
Adams Av ... P-13
Adams St ... L-18
Alabama St ... K-20
Alameda St ... K-M-11
Alamo St ... G-6
Alessandro Blvd ... L-19-20
Aliso Canyon Rd ... F-12
Alondra Blvd ... M-12
Alosta Av ... J-14
Altadena Dr ... H-12
Alton Av ... P-14
Alvarado St ... K-11
Anaheim St ... N-11
Angeles Crest Hwy ... F-16, H-12,G-14
Angeles Forest Hwy ... F-G-12
Antelope Rd ... N-20
Antonio Pkwy ... Q-16
Aqua Mansa Rd ... K-19
Archibald Av ... K-17
Arlington Av ... L-18
Armstrong Rd ... K-18
Arrow Blvd ... J-17
Arrow Hwy ... J-13-16
Arrowhead Lake Rd ... F-20
Arroyo Pkwy ... J-12
Artesia Blvd ... M-10-11
Artesia Frwy ... M-11
Avalon Blvd ... L-N-11
Aviation Blvd ... M-10
Azusa Av ... J-K-14

B
B St ... N-11
Bake Pkwy ... P-16
Balboa Blvd ... H-9,Q-14
Baldy Mesa Rd ... F-18
Ball Rd ... M-13
Barton Rd ... K-19
Base Line Av ... J-17
Base Line Rd ... J-15-20
Beach Blvd ... M-P-13
Beaumont Av ... L-22
Bell Grave Av ... L-16
Beverly Blvd ... K-10-12
Beverly Glen Blvd ... J-9
Big Pines Hwy ... F-15
Big Rock Creek Rd ... F-15
Birch St ... L-14
Bloomington Av ... J-18
Bob's Gap Rd ... F-14
Bolsa Chica St ... N-13
Bonita Canyon Dr ... P-14
Bowen Ranch Rd ... F-21
Brand Blvd ... H-9
Brea Blvd ... M-14
Brea Canyon Rd ... L-14
Bridge St ... M-21
Bristol St ... N-14
Brookhurst St ... M-P-13
Brookside Av ... K-20,L-22
Bryant St ... K-21
Burbank Blvd ... J-9

C
Cactus Av ... L-19
Cajalco Rd ... M-18-19
Cajon Blvd ... H-19
California Av ... L-17,N-21
California Blvd ... J-12
Cameron Av ... K-14
Carbon Canyon Rd ... L-15
Carmentia Rd ... L-13
Carson St ... M-12
Cedar Av ... K-18
Center St ... F-6,K-19
Centinela Blvd ... K-9
Central Av ... K-16, L-11-14-16-18
Century Blvd ... L-10
Chandler St ... L-16
Chapman Av ... N-13-15
Cherry Av ... J-17,L-22
Cherry Valley Blvd ... L-22
Chicago Av ... L-19
Chino Av ... K-16
Cima Mesa Rd ... F-13
Citrus Av ... J-18,K-20,L-17
Cleveland Av ... L-17
Cloverdale Rd ... L-17
Coldwater Canyon Av ... J-9
Colima Rd ... L-13-14
Colorado Blvd ... J-11
Columbia Av ... K-19
Commonwealth Av ... M-13, N-22
Compton Blvd ... M-11
Contour Av ... M-21
Coral Canyon Rd ... K-6
Corona Frwy ... L-16,N-18
Costa Mesa Frwy ... P-14
Crenshaw Blvd ... K-M-10
Crest Rd ... N-10
Creststone Rd ... K-18
Crown Valley Pkwy ... Q-16
Crown Valley Rd ... F-11
Crystal Creek Rd ... F-22
Culver Blvd ... L-9
Culver Dr ... P-15
Custer Av ... F-22

D
Davis Rd ... M-21
De Soto Av ... H-8
Del Amo Blvd ... M-12
Del Rosa Av ... J-20
Desert Front Rd ... F-16
Desert Lawn Dr ... L-21
Devils Punchbowl Rd ... F-14
Devonshire St ... H-8
Diamond Bar Blvd ... L-14
Duncan Canyon Rd ... J-18

E
E St ... J-19
Eaby Rd ... F-17
East Rd ... L-14
Eden Hot Springs Rd ... L-21
Edinger Av ... N-13-14
Edison Av ... K-16
El Prado Rd ... L-16
El Segundo Blvd ... L-10
El Sobrante Rd ... M-18
El Toro Rd ... P-16
Ellis Av ... N-19
Emerald Rd ... F-22
Escondido Frwy ... M-20
Esperanza Rd ... M-15
Esplanada Av ... N-22
Etiwanda Av ... K-17
Euclid Av ... K-L-16
Euclid St ... M-13,N-14

F
Fair Oaks Av ... J-12
Fairview Rd ... P-14
Fairview St ... N-14
Felipe Rd ... Q-16
Figueroa St ... J-M-11
Firestone Blvd ... L-12
Florence Av ... L-10
Florida Av ... N-21
Foothill Blvd ... J-13-14-16-18
Foothill Corridor ... P-16
Foothill Frwy ... H-10,J-12
Foothill Rd ... F-22
Fort Tejon Rd ... F-15
Francisquito Av ... K-13
Frederick Av ... L-20
Fullerton Rd ... L-14
Furnace Creek Rd ... F-22

G
Garden Grove Blvd ... N-13
Garden Grove Frwy ... N-13
Garey Av ... K-15
Gilman Springs ... L-21
Girard St ... N-22
Glendora Mountain Rd ... H-14
Glendora Ridge Rd ... H-15
Glenoaks Blvd ... H-10
Goetz Rd ... N-20
Golden West St ... N-13
Grand Av ... J-K-14,N-21
Grass Valley Rd ... H-20
Green Rd ... F-16
Green Valley Lake Rd ... H-21
Greenspot Rd ... J-20
Grove Av ... L-16

H
Hacienda Blvd ... L-13
Hammer Av ... K-L-17
Harbor Blvd ... L-14
Harbor Frwy ... L-M-10
Haven St ... J-17
Hawthorne Blvd ... M-10,N-9
Heacock St ... L-20
Hesperia Rd ... F-19
High Rd ... F-21
Highland Av ... J-18-19,L-9
Highland Springs Av ... L-22
Hillside Rd ... J-17
Hole Av ... L-18
Hollywood Frwy ... K-11
Hollywood Wy ... H-10
Holt Blvd ... K-16
Hubbard St ... G-9
Huntington Dr ... J-12-13,K-11

I
Idyllwild Dr ... M-22
Imperial Hwy ... L-13-14
Indian Hill Blvd ... K-15
Inland Ctr Dr ... J-19
Iris Av ... L-20
Iromona Blvd ... M-22
Irvine Blvd ... N-15
Irvine Center Dr ... P-15

J
J.F.K. Dr ... L-20
Jackrabbit Trail ... L-21
Jamboree Rd ... P-14
Jefferson Blvd ... L-9
Juniper Flats Rd ... N-21
Juniper Hills ... F-14
Jurupa Av ... K-18
Jurupa Rd ... K-18

K
Kanan Dume Rd ... K-6
Kanan Rd ... J-6
Katella Av ... N-12
Kendal Rd ... F-22
Kendall Dr ... J-19
Kiowa Rd ... F-20
Knott St ... N-13

L
La Brea Av ... K-10
La Cadena Dr ... K-19
La Cienega Blvd ... K-10
La Palma Av ... M-15
La Paz Rd ... Q-16
La Sierra Av ... L-17
La Tijera Blvd ... L-10
La Tuna Canyon Rd ... H-10
Laguna Canyon Rd ... Q-15
Lake Av ... J-12
Lake Gregory Dr ... H-19
Lakeview Av ... M-21
Lamb Canyon Rd ... M-22
Lambert Rd ... L-14
Lankershim Blvd ... H-10
Largo Vista Rd ... F-15
Las Virgenes Rd ... J-7
Laurel Canyon Blvd ... H-10
Leffingwell Rd ... L-13
Lime Canyon Rd ... F-6
Limonite St ... L-17
Lincoln Av ... M-13-17
Lincoln Blvd ... K-9
Linda Vista Av ... J-11
Lindero Canyon Rd ... J-6
Little Tujunga Rd ... G-10
Live Oak Canyon Rd ... P-16
Live Oak Dr ... J-13
Lone Pine Canyon Rd ... G-17
Long Beach Atlantic Blvd ... N-11
Long Beach Blvd ... L-11
Long Beach Frwy ... M-11
Lopez Canyon Rd ... G-9
Los Alamitos Blvd ... N-12
Los Alisos Blvd ... P-16
Los Angeles Av ... H-6
Los Feliz Blvd ... J-10
Los Flores Rd ... G-19
Lower Azusa Rd ... J-13
Lucretia Av ... L-17
Lugonia Av ... K-20
Lytle Creek Rd ... H-J-18

M
MacArthur ... Q-14
MacArthur Blvd ... P-14
Madera Rd ... H-6
Madison St ... L-18
Magic Mtn Pkwy ... F-8
Magnolia Av ... L-18
Manchester Av ... L-10
Maple Av ... F-19
Marguerite Pkwy ... Q-16
Markhan St ... M-19
Matthews Rd ... N-20
Mayberry Av ... N-22
McAllister St St ... M-18
McCall Blvd ... N-20
Menlo Av ... N-22
Merrill Av ... J-18,L-16
Mesa Av ... F-22
Mill Creek Rd ... H-22,J-21
Mill St ... J-19
Mills Av ... J-16
Mission Blvd ... K-15-17-18
Mockingbird Canyon Rd ... M-18
Montana Av ... K-9
Moody St ... M-13
Moreno Beach Dr ... L-20
Moreno Valley Frwy ... L-20
Moulton Pkwy ... Q-15
Mount Emma Rd ... F-12
Mountain Av ... J-K-16,N-22
Mountain Rd ... F-16
Mt Baldy Rd ... H-16
Mt Gleason Av ... H-10
Mt Vernon Av ... J-19
Muirlands Blvd ... P-16
Mulholland Dr ... J-8-9
Mulholland Hwy ... J-6
Myrtle Av ... J-13

N
Newport Frwy ... N-15
Nohl Ranch Rd ... M-15
Nordhoff St ... H-8
Normandie Av ... M-10
Norwalk Blvd ... L-12
Nuevo Av ... M-20

O
Oak Glen Rd ... K-21-22
Ocean Blvd ... N-11
Ocean Park Blvd ... K-9
Ocotillo Way ... F-21
Old Elsonora Rd ... M-19
Olive Av ... J-10
Olsen Rd ... H-6
Olympiad Rd ... P-16
Olympic Blvd ... K-9-10
Ontario Av ... M-17
Orange Frwy ... L-14
Orange St ... J-20
Ortega Hwy ... R-16
Osborne St ... H-10
Oso Pkwy ... Q-16

P
Pacific Av ... N-10
Pacific Coast Hwy ... K-5-8, M-10,P-3,Q-15
Pacific Park Dr ... Q-16
Pallett Creek Rd ... F-14
Palm Av ... J-20
Palos Verdes Dr S ... N-10
Palos Verdes Dr W ... N-9
Park Av ... N-22
Pasadena Frwy ... J-11
Pasco Del Mar ... N-10
Peach Av ... F-19
Peach St ... F-19
Peck Rd ... K-13
Pedley Rd ... L-18
Pennsylvania Av ... L-22
Pepper Av ... K-19
Perris Blvd ... M-20
Pershing Dr ... L-9
Phelon Rd ... F-17-18
Philadelphia St ... K-16
Pico Av ... N-20
Pierce St ... L-18
Pigeon Pass Rd ... K-19
Pinacate Rd ... N-21
Pine Av ... L-16
Pioneer Blvd ... M-12
Piuma Rd ... K-7
Polk St ... G-9
Pomona Blvd ... K-15
Pomona Frwy ... K-12-14-16
Portola Pkwy ... N-15
Post Office Rd ... F-22
Potter Dr ... M-22

R
Ramona Av ... K-16
Ramona Blvd ... K-13
Ramona Expwy ... M-20-21
Ramsey St ... L-22
Ranchero St ... F-19
Rancho Av ... K-19
Reche Canyon Rd ... K-19
Reche Vista Dr ... L-20
Redlands Blvd ... L-20
Redondo Beach Blvd ... M-10
Redondo Beach Frwy ... M-10
Reseda Blvd ... H-8
Rialto Blvd ... J-18
Rim of the World Dr ... H-22
Rinaldi St ... G-9
River St ... L-16
Riverside Av ... J-18-19
Riverside Dr ... K-16
Riverside Frwy ... L-M-14
Roberts Rd ... L-21
Rock Springs Rd ... F-20
Ronald Reagan Frwy ... H-6-8
Roscoe Blvd ... H-8
Rose Dr ... M-14
Rosecrans Av ... L-10-12
Rosemead ... L-12
Rosemead Blvd ... K-12
Roundup Way ... F-20
Royal Av ... H-6

S
San Bernardino Av ... K-17-20
San Bernardino Frwy ... K-11-14-18-22
San Diego Frwy ... J-9,M-10, N-13,Q-16
San Dimas Canyon Rd ... J-15
San Dimas Av ... J-15
San Fernando Rd ... F-8, H-9,J-10
San Gabriel Blvd ... J-12
San Gabriel Canyon Rd ... J-14
San Gabriel River Frwy ... J-13,L-12
San Jacinto St ... N-22
San Joaquin Hills Corridor ... Q-15
San Timoteo Rd ... K-20
San Vente Blvd ... K-9
Sand Canyon Av ... P-15
Sand Canyon Rd ... F-9
Sanderson Av ... M-22
Santa Ana Frwy ... K-11, M-13,N-15
Santa Fe Rd E ... F-19
Santa Monica Blvd ... J-10,K-9
Santa Monica Frwy ... K-9
Santa Rosa Rd ... N-19
Santa Susana Pass Rd ... H-7
Santiago Canyon Rd ... N-15-16
Seal Beach Blvd ... N-12
Seaside Blvd ... N-11
Seco Canyon Rd ... F-8
Segerstrom Av ... P-14
Sepulveda Blvd ... H-M-9,N-11
Seven Oaks Rd ... H-22
Shaver St ... N-22
Sherman Way ... H-8
Sierra Av ... J-18
Sierra Madre Av ... J-14
Sierra Madre Blvd ... J-12
Silverado Canyon Rd ... N-16
Simpson Av ... N-21
Simpson Rd ... N-21
Singleton Rd ... L-21
Slater Av ... P-13
Slauson Av ... L-10
Slover Av ... K-18
Smith Rd ... F-17
Soboba Rd ... M-22
Soledad Canyon Rd ... F-8-10
South St ... M-12
Spring St ... M-12
St College Blvd ... M-14
Stanford St ... N-22
State St ... J-19,N-22
Stetson Av ... N-22
Sugar Loaf Truck Trail ... H-22
Summit Rd ... G-18
Sunland Blvd ... H-10
Sunset Av ... K-13
Sunset Blvd ... J-10,K-9

T
Talbert Av ... P-13
Tampa Av ... H-8
Tapo Canyon Rd ... G-7
Telegraph Rd ... F-6
Terminal Frwy ... N-11
Theodore St ... L-21
Thousand Oaks Blvd ... J-6
Tierra Rejada Rd ... H-6
Timoteo Canyon Rd ... L-21
Tippecanoe Av ... K-19
Topanga Canyon Blvd ... J-8
Towne Av ... J-K-15
Trade Post Rd ... F-22
Trautwein Rd ... L-19
Triunfo Canyon Rd ... J-6
Tulip Ln ... H-22
Turnbull Canyon Rd ... L-13
Tyler St ... L-18

U
University Av ... L-19

V
Valley Blvd ... K-12-13-14-18
Valley of the Falls Dr ... J-22
Valley View St ... L-N-13
Valley Vista Av ... F-20
Van Buren Blvd ... K-17,M-19
Van Nuys Blvd ... H-9
Vasquez Canyon Rd ... F-9
Venice Blvd ... K-9-10
Ventura ... J-9
Ventura Blvd ... J-9
Ventura Frwy ... J-7
Vermont Av ... K-10
Vernon Av ... K-10
Victoria Av ... L-18
Victory Blvd ... H-8-9
Vincent Av ... J-14
Vineyard Av ... K-16
Vista Del Mar ... L-9

W
Warner Av ... N-14
Warren Rd ... M-22
Washington Blvd ... J-K-12
Waterman Av ... J-19
Wentworth St ... H-10
Western Av ... K-N-10
Westlake Blvd ... J-6
Westminster Av ... N-13
Whittier Blvd ... K-12,L-13
Wildwood Canyon Rd ... K-22
Wilmington Blvd ... M-11
Wilshire Blvd ... K-9-10
Wilson Ranch Rd ... F-17
Winnetka Av ... H-8
Woodhouse Rd ... L-21
Workman Mill Rd ... K-13
Wren St ... F-20

Y
Yorba Linda Blvd ... M-15
Yucaipa Blvd ... K-21

CITIES & TOWNS
Acton ... F-11
Agoura Hills ... J-6
Alberhill ... N-18
Alhambra ... K-12
Alta Loma ... J-16
Altadena ... H-12
Anaheim ... M-14
Angelus Oaks ... J-22
Arcadia ... J-13
Arleta ... H-9
Arrowbear Lake ... H-21
Artesia ... M-12
Atwood ... M-15
Azusa ... J-14
Balboa ... Q-14
Baldwin Park ... J-13
Baldy Mesa ... F-18
Beaumont ... L-22
Bel Air ... K-9
Bell ... L-11
Bell Gardens ... L-12
Bellflower ... M-12
Belltown ... K-18
Beverly Glen ... J-9
Beverly Hills ... J-9
Big Bear Lake ... H-22
Bloomington ... K-18
Blue Jay ... H-20
Bolsa ... N-13
Bradbury ... J-13
Brea ... L-14
Brentwood Heights ... K-9
Bryn Mawr ... K-20
Buena Park ... M-13
Burbank ... H-10
Cajon Junction ... G-18
Calabasas ... J-7
Calimesa ... K-21
Canoga Park ... H-8
Capistrano Beach ... R-16
Carson ... M-11
Cedar Glen ... H-20
Cedarpines Park ... H-19
Cerritos ... M-13
Chapman Woods ... J-12
Charter Oak ... J-14
Chatsworth ... H-8
Cherry Valley ... L-22
Chino ... K-16
Chino Hills ... L-15
City of Industry ... K-13
Claremont ... J-15
Colton ... K-19
Commerce ... K-12
Compton ... M-11
Cornell ... J-6
Corona ... M-17
Corona Del Mar ... Q-14
Coronita ... M-17
Costa Mesa ... P-14
Coto De Caza ... P-17
Covina ... K-14
Cowan Heights ... N-15
Crafton ... K-21
Crest Park ... H-20
Crestline ... H-19
Crestmore ... K-18
Crystal Cove ... Q-14
Cudahy ... L-11
Culver City ... K-9
Cypress ... M-13
Dana Point ... R-16
Devore ... H-18
Diamond Bar ... L-15
Downey ... L-12
Duarte ... J-13
East Highlands ... J-20
East Los Angeles ... K-12
East Pasadena ... J-12
East San Gabriel ... J-12
East Tustin ... N-15
El Casco Lake ... L-21
El Cerrito ... M-17
El Modena ... N-15
El Monte ... K-13
El Nido ... M-10
El Porto Beach ... M-9
El Segundo ... L-9
Emerald Bay ... Q-15
Encino ... J-9
Fawnskin ... H-22
Fernwood ... K-8
Florence ... L-11
Fontana ... J-17
Fountain Valley ... P-13
Fullerton ... M-14
Garden Grove ... N-13
Gardena ... M-10
Gilman Hot Springs ... M-22
Glen Avon ... K-17
Glendale ... J-11
Glendora ... J-14
Glenview ... J-8
Graham ... L-11
Granada Hills ... H-8
Grand Terrace ... K-19
Green Valley Lake ... H-21
Guasti ... K-17
Hacienda Hts ... L-13
Harbor City ... N-10
Hawaiian Gardens ... M-12
Hawthorne ... L-10
Hemet ... N-22
Hermosa Beach ... M-9
Hesperia ... F-19
Hidden Hills ... J-7
Highgrove ... K-19
Highland ... J-20
Hollywood ... J-10
Home Gardens ... M-17
Homeland ... N-21
Huntington Beach ... N-13
Huntington Harbor ... N-12
Huntington Park ... L-11
Inglewood ... L-10
Irvine ... P-15
Irwindale ... J-14
Juniper Hills ... F-14
Juniper Springs ... N-21
La Canada Flintridge ... H-11
La Crescenta ... H-11
La Habra ... L-13
La Habra Hts ... L-13
La Mirada ... L-13
La Palma ... M-13
La Puente ... K-13
La Verne ... J-15
Ladera Heights ... L-10
Laguna Beach ... Q-15
Laguna Hills ... Q-16
Laguna Niguel ... R-16
Lake Arrowhead ... H-20
Lake Forest ... P-16
Lakeview ... M-21
Lakewood ... M-12
Lawndale ... M-10
Lemon Heights ... N-15
Lennox ... L-10
Loma Linda ... K-20
Lomita ... N-10
Long Beach ... N-12
Los Alamitos ... N-12
Los Angeles ... K-8
Los Nietos ... L-12
Los Serranos ... L-16
Lucerne Valley ... F-22
Lynwood ... L-11
Lytle Creek ... H-17
Malibu ... K-7
Manhattan Beach ... M-9
Marina Del Rey ... L-9
Maywood ... L-11
Mentone ... K-21
Midway City ... N-13
Mill Creek Park ... J-22
Mira Loma ... K-17
Mission Hills ... H-9
Mission Viejo ... Q-16
Modjeska ... N-16
Monrovia ... H-13
Montclair ... K-16
Montebello ... K-12
Monterey Park ... K-12
Moreno Valley ... L-20
Mount Baldy ... H-16
Muscoy ... J-19
Newhall ... G-8
Newhall Ranch ... F-8
Newport Beach ... Q-14
Norco ... L-17
North Hollywood ... J-10
North Long Beach ... M-11
Northridge ... H-8
Norwalk ... M-12
Nuevo ... M-21
Olinda ... L-15
Olive ... M-14
Ontario ... K-16
Orange ... N-14
Orange Park Acres ... N-15
Pacific Palisades ... K-8
Pacoima ... H-9
Palos Verdes Estates ... N-10
Paramount ... M-11
Pasadena ... J-12
Pedley ... L-18
Perris ... M-20
Phelon ... F-17
Pico Rivera ... K-12
Pinon Hills ... F-16
Piru ... F-6
Placentia ... M-14
Playa Del Rey ... L-9
Pomona ... K-15
Porter Ranch ... G-8
Rancho Cucamonga ... J-16
Rancho Palos Verdes ... N-10
Rancho San Margarita ... P-17
Red Hill ... N-15
Redlands ... K-20
Redondo Beach ... M-9
Reseda ... H-8
Rialto ... J-18
Rimforest ... H-20
Riverside ... L-19
Rolling Hills ... N-10
Rolling Hills Estates ... N-10
Romoland ... N-20
Rosemead ... K-12
Rossmoor ... N-12
Rowland Heights ... L-14
Rubidoux ... J-18
Running Springs ... H-21
San Antonio Heights ... J-16
San Bernardino ... J-19
San Clemente ... R-16
San Dimas ... J-15
San Fernando ... G-9
San Gabriel ... J-12
San Jacinto ... N-22
San Juan Capistrano ... R-16
San Marino ... J-12
San Pedro ... N-10
Santa Ana ... N-14
Santa Clarita ... F-8
Santa Fe Springs ... L-13
Santa Monica ... K-8
Saugus ... F-8
Scotland ... H-17
Seal Beach ... N-12
Sepulveda ... H-9
Sherman Oaks ... J-9
Sierra Madre ... J-13
Signal Hill ... N-12
Silverado ... N-16
Simi Valley ... G-6
Skyforest ... H-20
Sleepy Hollow ... L-15
Solemint ... F-9
South El Monte ... K-13
South Fontana ... K-18
South Gate ... L-11
South Laguna ... R-15
South Pasadena ... J-12
South San Gabriel ... K-12
South San Jose Hills ... K-14
South Whittier ... L-13
Stanton ... N-13
Studio City ... J-9
Summit ... G-18
Sun City ... N-20
Sun Valley ... H-10
Sunland ... H-10
Sunnyslope ... K-18
Sunset Beach ... P-13
Surfside ... N-12
Sylmar ... G-9
Sylvia Park ... J-8
Tarzana ... J-8
Temple City ... J-12
Three Arch Bay ... R-16
Topanga ... J-8
Topanga Beach ... K-8
Topanga Park ... J-7
Torrance ... M-10
Tujunga ... H-10
Tustin ... N-15
Twin Peaks ... H-20
Upland ... J-16
Val Verde ... F-7
Valinda ... K-13
Valyermo ... F-15
Van Nuys ... H-9
Venice ... L-9
Verdemont ... H-19
Vernon ... K-11
View Park ... K-10
Villa Park ... M-15
Walnut ... K-14
Walnut Park ... L-11
West Athens ... L-10
West Carson ... M-10
West Covina ... K-14
West Hollywood ... K-10
West Los Angeles ... K-9
West Puente Valley ... K-13
West Whittier ... L-12
Westlake Village ... J-6
Westminster ... N-13
Westmont ... L-10
Whittier ... L-13
Willow Brook ... L-11
Winchester ... N-21
Windsor Hills ... L-10
Woodcrest ... M-19
Woodland Hills ... J-8
Wrightwood ... G-16
Yorba Linda ... M-15

PARKS & GOLF COURSES
Aliso Wood Canyons Regional Park ... Q-15
Arcadia Park ... J-13
Arroyo Seco Park ... J-11
Big Dalton Wilderness Park ... J-14
Bolsa Chica State Beach ... P-13
Bolsa Chica Wetlands (Ecological Res) ... P-13
Bonelli Regional Park ... K-15
Box Springs Mountain Regional Park ... L-19
Brand Park ... H-11
Cabrillo Beach Park ... P-11
California Citrus State Historical Park ... M-18
Centennial Park ... N-14
Chino Hills State Park ... L-16
Cleveland National Forest ... N-16
Colonial Golf Course ... N-22
Corona Del Mar State Beach ... Q-14
Crystal Cove State Park ... Q-15
Cucamonga Wilderness ... H-17
Dan Blocker State Beach ... K-6
Deukmejian Wilderness Park ... H-11
Dockweiler State Beach ... L-9
Doheny State Beach ... R-16
El Dorado Park ... M-12
Elysian Park ... K-11
Fairmount Park ... K-18
Glen Helen Regional Park ... H-18
Hansen Dam Park ... H-10
Huntington State Beach ... P-13
Irvine Park ... N-15
Jessup Park ... H-9
Jurupa Hills Regional Park ... K-18
Laguna Niguel Regional Park ... Q-16
Lake Perris State Recreation Area ... M-20
Limestone Canyon Regional Park ... N-16
Los Encinos State Historical Park ... J-9
Lower Arroyo Park ... J-11
Malibu Creek State Park ... K-6
Malibu Lagoon State Beach ... K-7
Manhattan State Beach ... M-9
Marshall Canyon Regional Park ... J-15
Mile Square Park ... N-13
Monrovia Mountain Park ... J-13
Moreno Valley Ranch ... M-20
O'Melveny Park ... G-8
O'Neill Park ... P-16
Peck Park ... N-10
Placerita Canyon State Park ... G-9
Point Dume State Beach ... K-6
Recreation Park ... N-12
Redlands Golf Course ... K-21
Reseda Park ... H-8
Roy Kabian Memorial Park ... N-20
San Bernardino National Forest ... H-18
San Gabriel Wilderness ... G-14
San Onofre State Park ... R-17
Santa Monica Mountains National Recreation Area ... J-7
Santa Monica State Beach ... L-9
Sepulved Dam Recreation Area ... J-8
Seven Hills Golf Course ... N-22
Silverwood Lake State Recreation Area ... G-19
Soboba Springs Golf Course ... M-22
South Hills Park ... J-14
Sycamore Canyon Park ... L-19
Topanga State Park ... J-8
Torba Reg Park ... M-15
Veterans Memorial Park ... G-9
Villa Park Dam Regional Park ... M-15
White Oaks Park ... G-7
Wildwood Canyon Park ... H-10
Will Rogers State Beach ... K-8
Will Rogers State Historical Park ... K-8
William Mason Regional Park ... P-15

POINTS OF INTEREST
Apple White Campground ... H-17
Armed Forces Reserve Center ... N-13
Basin Campground ... F-13
Blockbuster Pavilion Amphitheatre ... H-18
Brackett Field ... J-15
Buckhorn Ski Area ... G-14
Burbank-Glendale Pasadena Airport ... H-10
Cable Airport ... J-16
Cajon Campground ... G-18
Carousel Mall ... J-19
Chamber of Commerce (Hemet) ... N-22
Chamber of Commerce (Moreno Valley) ... L-19
Chamber of Commerce (Redlands) ... K-20
Chamber of Commerce (Riverside) ... L-18
Chamber of Commerce (San Bernardino) ... J-19
Chantry Flat Campground ... H-13
Charleton Flat Campground ... G-13
Chilao Campground ... G-13
Chino Airport ... L-16
Civic Center (Hemet) ... N-22
Coldbrook Campground ... G-14
Compton Airport ... M-11
Convention and Visitors Bureau (San Bernardino) ... J-19
Convention Center (Riverside) ... K-19
Corona Municipal Airport ... M-17
Crystal Lake Campground ... G-14
Deep Creek Campground ... G-20
Devore Campground ... H-13
Disneyland ... M-14
Dodger Stadium ... K-11
Dogwood Campground ... H-20
Cedars-Sinai Medical Center ... K-10
El Monte Airport ... K-13
El Toro MCAS ... P-15
Empire Center ... K-18
Ft MacArthur Military Reservation ... P-10
Galleria at Tyler ... L-18
Glacier Campground ... H-16
Glen Ivy Hot Springs Campground ... N-17
Government Center ... J-19
Grout Bay Campground ... H-22
Hawthorne Municipal Airport ... L-10
Hemet Valley Medical Center ... N-22
Historic Mission Inn ... L-19
Historic Municipal Auditorium ... L-19
Inland Shop Center ... J-19
John Wayne Airport (Orange Co) ... P-14
Kaiser Foundation Hospital ... J-18
Kaiser Foundation Hospital Riverside ... L-18
Kratka Ridge Ski Area ... G-14
Long Beach Airport ... M-12
Los Angeles International Airport ... L-9
Lower Trabuco Campground ... P-17
March Air Reserve Base ... M-19
Moreno Valley Mall ... L-19
Mount Baldy Ski Area ... G-16
Mount Waterman Ski Area ... G-14
Mount Wilson Observatory ... H-12
Mountain High Ski Area ... F-16
National Orange Show Grounds ... J-19
North Shore Campground ... G-20
Ontario Int'l Airport ... K-17
Pacific Crest National Scenic Trail ... G-16-20
Pappy Keef Campground ... F-11
Parkview Community Hospital Medical Center ... L-18
Patton State Hospital ... J-20
Pine Campground ... H-12
Redlands Municipal Airport ... J-20
Rialto Municipal Airport ... J-18
Riverside Community Hospital ... L-18
Riverside Flabob Airport ... L-18
Riverside General Hospital University Medical Center ... L-18
Riverside Municipal Airport ... L-18
Riverside Plaza ... L-18
Riverside Sports Center ... L-19
Riverside Sports Complex ... K-19
Rose Bowl ... J-12
San Bernardino Community Hospital ... J-19
San Bernardino International Airport ... J-20
San Manuel Indian Reservation ... J-20
Santa Ana MCAS Campground ... P-15
Santa Fe Trail 1849 Monument ... G-18
Santa Monica Municipal Airport ... K-9
Six Flags Magic Mountain ... F-8
Ski Green Valley Ski Area ... H-21
Ski Sunrise Ski Area ... F-16
Snow Valley Ski Area ... J-21
Spruce Grove Campground ... H-13
St. Bernardino Medical Center ... J-19
Switzer Campground ... H-12
Toll Road Campground ... G-20
Torrance Municipal Airport ... N-10
UCLA Medical Center ... M-10
United States Naval Reservation ... N-10
United States Naval Weapons Station ... N-12
Universal City ... J-10
Valencia Town Center Mall ... F-8
Valley Forge Campground ... H-12
Van Nuys Airport ... H-9
Veterans Medical Center ... K-9
Vista Campground ... G-13
Whiteman Airport ... H-9

SCHOOLS
Biola University ... L-13
California Baptist College ... L-18
California State University Fullerton ... M-14
California State University Los Angeles ... K-11
California State University Northridge ... H-8
California State University San Bernardino ... H-19
Cypress College ... M-13
Irvine Valley College ... P-15
Loma Linda University ... K-19
Los Angeles Sierra University ... L-17
Loyola Marymount University ... L-9
Pepperdine University ... K-7
St. Marys College ... K-9
UCLA ... K-9
University of California Exp Station ... L-19
University of California Irvine ... P-14
University of California Riverside ... L-19
University of Redlands ... K-20
University Southern California ... K-10
West Coast University ... K-10
West Los Angeles College ... K-10
Whittier College ... L-13
Woodbury University ... H-10

77075431-67
9780528981654
APEX
TP